Skills
Writing and Grammar

Martha O'Dell

OXFORD

OXFORD
UNIVERSITY PRESS

Great Clarendon Street, Oxford, OX2 6DP, United Kingdom

Oxford University Press is a department of the University of Oxford. It furthers the University's objective of excellence in research, scholarship, and education by publishing worldwide. Oxford is a registered trade mark of Oxford University Press in the UK and in certain other countries.

British Library Cataloguing in Publication Data
Data available

9781382046145

10 9 8 7 6 5 4 3 2 1

Paper used in the production of this book is a natural, recyclable product made from wood grown in sustainable forests.

The manufacturing process conforms to the environmental regulations of the country of origin.

Printed in China by Golden Cup

Acknowledgements
The publisher and authors would like to thank the following for permission to use photographs and other copyright material:

Cover: Andrea Manzati

Photos: p8: Zhuravleva Katia/Shutterstock: p6: MM Studios: p10: Mark Mason: p12: Ermolaev Alexander/Shutterstock: p14: Joop Hoek/Shutterstock: p16: Andrii Iemelianenko/Shutterstock: p22: frankvessia/Shutterstock: p24: home/Shutterstock: p26: Pixsooz/Shutterstock: p28: formatoriginal/Vecteezy: p30 (l): Prostock-studi/Shutterstock: p30 (r): Gareth Boden: p32: Hurst Photo/Shutterstock: p34: solarseven/123RF: p36: Amelia Martin/Shutterstock: p38: koko-tewan/Shutterstock: p40: Elnur/Shutterstock: p42: Artenauta Images/Shutterstock: p44: fizkes/Shutterstock: p46: LittlePerfectStock/Shutterstock: p48: Unholy Vault Designs/Shutterstock: p50: BONDART PHOTOGRAPHY/Shutterstock: p52: hoshinosuu/Shutterstock: p54: Lane Oatey/Blue Jean Images/Corbis: p56: CREATISTA/Shutterstock: p58: Jacob Lund/Shutterstock: p60: Prostock-studi/Shutterstock: p62: lassedesignen/Shutterstock: p64 (t): Yulia Glam/Shutterstock: p64 (b): Yulia Glam/Shutterstock: p66: Muzhik/Shutterstock: 70: marina/Shutterstock: p68: AnyaPL/Shutterstock: p72: Rawpixel.com/Shutterstock: p74: Valeriy Kachaev/Alamy Stock Vector

Artwork by Andrew Painter; Paul Daviz; Oxford University Press; Oxford University Press ANZ; QBS Learning

Every effort has been made to contact copyright holders of material reproduced in this book. Any omissions will be rectified in subsequent printings if notice is given to the publisher.

Contents

1 Take turns with a partner:

- Think of a simple object (for example, a house, tree or car) – but don't tell your partner what it is.
- Give your partner step-by-step instructions on how to draw the object. (For example, 'First draw a square in the middle of the box, leaving space around the edges … ')
- Finished? Can your partner tell what the object is?
- Could the instructions have been clearer? How?

2 Complete the sentences with the correct **imperatives**.

| Remember to | Careful | Don't | forget | ~~Put~~ | Arrive | be |

Put your plate on the counter when you have finished lunch.

a Never _________________________ to put your rubbish in the bin.

b _________________________ allow enough time to eat lunch.

c _________________________ dive into the shallow end of the pool.

d Please _________________________ quiet during the movie.

e _________________________ five minutes early so you have time to change into your sports kit.

f _________________________ ! The floor can be slippery when wet.

3 Think of something you do regularly that involves a series of steps. (For example: choosing your lunch at school, taking a book out of the library, attending a club, going out with family.) Imagine you are giving instructions on how to do this to a young person who has just arrived in the country. What are the key steps they need to know? Make notes below.

4 Now write your instructions using imperatives and bullet points.

When you've finished, underline the imperatives you have used.

1 Discuss with a partner:

- What are your favourite dishes?
- What dishes can you cook?
- Have you ever had a great success in the kitchen? Have you ever had a disaster?
- Do you follow recipes or make them up?

2 Complete the recipe instructions with these dynamic verbs.

~~put~~	pour	beat	fry	mash	melt

Divide the mixture equally between the tins and   put   into a preheated oven for 20 minutes.

a Gently ___________________ the onion in the melted fat.

b ___________________ the fish and butter together with a fork.

c ___________________ the liquid over the fish fillets and leave to marinate overnight.

d ___________________ the butter in a large saucepan.

e ___________________ the egg whites until they are frothy.

3 Most recipes start with a description to appeal to the reader. Match the **language device** used with a technique from the box.

power of three	simile	alliteration	rhetorical question	~~sensory imagery~~

Using melted chocolate instead of cocoa powder gives this sponge a wonderfully fudgy texture.
   sensory imagery

a It's got beautifully succulent chicken, crunchy veg, and a sweet and sour hit from the

grilled pineapple – delicious! ___________________

b On hot summer evenings, it's hard to turn down a sweet, juicy nectarine, but what

about adding it to everyone's favourite salad? ___________________

c This angel cake will be light as a feather if you whisk the mixture thoroughly. ___________________

d These super sweet chilli spring rolls are a simple savoury snack. ___________________

4 Write your favourite recipe. Include:

- a short description of the meal to appeal to the reader (include the language devices from **3**)
- dynamic verbs in the method.

When finished, circle the dynamic verbs you have used.

1 Discuss with a partner:

- Do you have a good sense of direction? Do you ever get lost?
- If you are lost, do you prefer to ask someone for directions or use a map or phone? Why?
- What is the hardest thing about giving directions to someone?

2 Circle the correct **prepositions** in these directions.

Walk along/at the road until you reach the school.

a Go under/between the bridge, being careful not to step in a puddle.

b Walk of/from the school to the roundabout.

c Walk against/across the park to the gate on the other side.

d Travel towards/for the centre on foot.

e Turn left in/at the junction.

3 Using the map above, write directions for each journey. Include prepositional phrases.

a From your house to school.

b From school to your friend's house.

c From your friend's house to your parent's office.

4 Imagine an exchange student is staying at your house.

- Write detailed directions to help them get to your school and your favourite places, such as the park, the cinema or the sports hall.
- Include different ways to get around and say how long each journey will take.
- Remember to use prepositional phrases.

There are lots of great places to visit in our town, some of them you can walk to …

When finished, underline any prepositional phrases you have used.

1 Discuss with a partner:

- How often do your teachers ask you to write definitions?
- In which subjects do you need to write definitions?
- Do you find it easy to write definitions?
- Are there some words that are hard to define?

2 Complete the sentences using these relative pronouns.

> where   which   who

This is the spot   *where*   I like to read.

a Are you the one ________________ sent me the text message?

b Is that the place ________________ I should meet you?

c The woman ________________ called said she would ring again.

d Where's the book ________________ Paola lent you?

e A rod is an object ________________ is used for fishing.

3 a Write a definition for each of the following using 'where', 'which' or 'who'. Do not write down the name of what you are describing!

- something in your bedroom

  This is an object which I use to help me wake up in the mornings.

- something in the classroom

  ____

- somewhere in your town or city

  ____

- something you would find in a supermarket

  ____

- somewhere in the school

  ____

- someone who everyone in your country knows

  ____

b When finished, read out your definitions to your partner and see if they can guess what the object, place or person is.

4 Play the false definitions game with a partner. Decide who will be Player A and who will be Player B. For each word in your box, write two definitions that are false, and one definition that is true (use a dictionary if you need to). Use **relative clauses** in your definitions.

'Lollygag' is

1. a name for a person who is very lazy

2. a shop where lots of different sweets are sold

3. a verb which means to spend time aimlessly [TRUE]

Player A: gravy boat   nibling   snollygoster

Player B: diphthong   whipper snapper   galley

When you have finished, read your definitions to your partner. See if they can guess which is the real definition. Then underline any relative clauses you have used.

1. Discuss with a partner:
   - What are the benefits of house sitting (looking after someone else's house while they are away)? Consider both the house sitter (the person who looks after the house) and the home owner.
   - What tasks would a house sitter do?
   - What qualities would a good house sitter have?

2. Write an advert for a house sitter to look after your house for three weeks. Include the main responsibilities and a description of the kind of person you're looking for.

Useful phrases
- We are looking for …
- The ideal candidate will have …
- Duties and responsibilities will include …
- The house sitter will also be responsible for …
- Apply by …

3. Here are some instructions for a house sitter. Identify the type of noun in each sentence.

> proper noun   concrete noun   irregular plural noun   abstract noun   ~~uncountable noun~~

Please take out the <u>rubbish</u> every week; it is collected on Thursdays.   *uncountable noun*

a. In case of an emergency, please call us or contact our neighbour, <u>Farida</u>.

b. Please feed the <u>fish</u> every morning. The food is under the sink.

c. Please make sure you lock the <u>front door</u> every time you leave the house.

d. I think you will find that our neighbourhood is very quiet, so we hope you will enjoy the <u>peace</u>.

4   Write detailed instructions for your house sitter. Include information on:

- pet care (invent pets if you don't have them)
- making the house secure, such as locks or alarms
- cleaning
- what to do in an emergency.

Use subheadings and bullet points if you like.

When finished, see if you can circle a proper noun, an abstract noun, a concrete noun, an uncountable noun and a noun with an irregular plural. If not, try to add the missing ones.

1 Discuss with a partner:

- What do you need to do to live a healthy life?
- How often do you do these things?
- What can stop people from living healthy lives?

2 Circle the **modal verbs** in these sentences about healthy living.

Teenagers need a lot of sleep. You should sleep for 8–10 hours a night.

a Turning off your phone or the TV while you do homework may help you get it finished faster!

b To stay healthy, we must eat a healthy diet including fruit and vegetables.

c More regular exercise would have a positive impact on my mental health.

d You could try to drink more water, to see if that helps you concentrate better in class.

3 Complete the sentences with a modal verb from the box. More than one answer is possible. Try to use a different modal verb in each space!

~~can~~	should	would	must	could	may	might

I know you   *can*   play football, I saw you at the park.

a I _________________ be more organized if my bedroom was tidy, but I don't always put everything away.

b If I got extra tuition, it _________________ help my school grades.

c If I practised the piano more, I _________________ be able to join a band.

d If I learned more about science, I think I _________________ enjoy it more.

e To be happy in life, you _________________ slow down and take time to enjoy it.

Now write two more sentences using modal verbs.

____

____

____

____

4 Write an article about the difference between what people know they *should* do and what they *actually* do in life. You could write about anything – healthy living, school work, helping the family, music or sports practice. Use modal verbs.

At the weekend most students have homework to do for school. They know that they should try to do it at the start of the weekend, so it's finished and they can enjoy themselves, but …

Tick off each modal verb that you have used:

☐ must   ☐ can   ☐ will   ☐ could   ☐ should   ☐ might   ☐ would   ☐ may

1   Discuss with a partner:

What are the advantages and disadvantages of using each type of narrator?

- First person (a story told through the use of the pronoun 'I')
- **Third person** (a story told through the use of the pronoun 'he' or 'she')
- Third person omniscient (a narrator who sees and knows everything that happens in the story)

2   Underline the pronouns in the following sentences.

Call me Ishmael.

a   Before I was two years old, something happened which I have never forgotten.

b   First, she tried to look down and make out what she was coming to, but it was too dark to see anything.

c   She sat with her feet tucked under her, and leaned against her father, who held her in his arm.

d   The bowls never wanted washing. The boys polished them with their spoons till they shone again.

3   With a partner, discuss these two narrators. Who are they? How are they connected? Note down your thoughts.

> I was tired, but not ready to go to sleep. It had been an eventful day and thoughts whirled around my mind, so I sat staring out into the darkness. The moon was large and low, more yellow than usual. It had a friendly look to it that I'd never noticed before.

> I'm never alone, not really. The Earth and I, we spin together. I can see so much, the whole blue and green planet, but also small things, a tree bending in the wind, a young man, staring up at me. I'm never alone, not really.

4 **a** On a separate piece of paper, write down some ideas for each of these situations and the unusual narrative perspectives:

- Someone being attacked by a bee: write from the perspective of the bee.
- Someone eating a sandwich: write from the perspective of the sandwich.
- Someone viewing a portrait of a past king or queen: write from the perspective of the portrait.

    b Choose your favourite and describe the scene from the unusual perspective.

When finished, underline the pronouns you have used.

1 Discuss with a partner:

- Which famous films or stories do you know where the main character is involved in a dramatic action scene?
- What types of settings do these scenes take place in?
- Why do you think these stories are so popular?

2 Choose the correct verb for each sentence. Then decide if the verb is dynamic (like 'jump') or stative (like 'think', 'see' or 'be'). Write (D) or (S).

> believe   hit   understand   need   like   ~~ride~~

I   ride   my bike to school every day.   (D)

a When we go to the beach, we ________________ to surf. ______

b I find it hard to ________________ some subjects at school. ______

c After that long run, I ________________ a glass of water. ______

d We watched the tennis match. Venus ________________ the ball really hard. ______

e My grandmother could not ________________ how tall I'd grown. ______

3 Short sentences can be used to create tension (a feeling of fear or excitement). Rewrite these texts to include a short sentence. Then circle the dynamic and stative verbs.

Her heart beat fast as she edged along the narrow rock ledge and she tried not to look down.

Her heart (beat) fast as she (edged) along the narrow rock ledge. She (tried) not to (look) down.

a Struggling to his feet again, Lu raced down the narrow path towards the finish line and he knew in his heart that he could win the race.

____

____

____

b The two friends swam out as far as they could, until the beach was just a dot in the distance and then, suddenly, Mohammed saw a fin from the corner of his eye – was it a shark?

____

____

4 Write an action scene. You can use a character from a film or a story, or invent your own. Remember to use dynamic verbs and short sentences. Don't let your hero escape too easily!

When finished, circle any dynamic verbs you have used and underline the short sentences.

1 With a partner, can you think of **metaphors** to connect these pictures? Use the words below to help you.

| wolf | sunny | lone | wave of | smile | terror |

2 Underline the metaphor and circle the **personification** in these sentences.

He awoke in a fog of uncertainty, the light overhead staring down at him.

a The stars were diamonds, scattered across the sky, peering down at the cities below.

b The waves crashed angrily against the shore, the surrounding cliffs are silent statues.

c In the vibrant town of Metaphoria, every street is paved with words and every building tells a tale.

d Their exhaustion was a heavy weight, but the mountain called to them, they had to go on …

e They struggled across the endless blank canvas of the desert under the relentless gaze of the scorching sun.

3 Choose one of these story ideas or think of your own and then make notes about what will happen.

Two 14-year-olds …
- walk and climb through jagged mountains on a mission to reach the highest peak …
- navigate a bustling city to find their friend …
- search for a hidden key in a wide-open field, desert or beach …

4   Write the opening of your story using your ideas from **3**. Include metaphors and personification to grab your reader's attention and help them picture the scene.

When finished, underline any metaphors you have used and circle any personification.

1 Discuss with a partner:

- Have you ever kept a diary?
- Do you like writing emails or letters? What about reading them?
- Can you think of any books in which the story is told through letters, emails or diary entries?
- How is it different to other types of stories?
- Why do people like reading this type of fiction?

2 There are seven **adverbs of time** in this diary entry. The first has been found. Circle the other six.

Dear Diary,

Yesterday, something very strange indeed happened! I slept late and woke up in a bit of a blur, but it was not until I opened the blinds and looked out, that I noticed the sky had turned a bright orange colour. First, I was amazed but then I decided to go out and investigate.

Once I had dressed, I ran out on the street to get a closer look. The sky looked even more orange and my neighbours began to say that something strange had happened last night …

3 Heroes usually alter or change during the narrative. Discuss with a partner how a character might change in the following situations and make notes about your ideas.

a Your character is very shy but secretly wants to be an entertainer. They audition for the lead role in the school show.

b Your character is a very 'indoor' person but wins an adventure holiday. Activities include bungee jumping, kayaking and camping in a jungle.

c Your character is very lazy and can't do anything for themselves. However, they have to look after their young cousins for the weekend.

4 Choose one of the characters and situations from **3**. Write three diary entries for the character. Try to show the character changing in some way.

When finished, underline any adverbs/adverbials of time you have used.

1 With a partner, take turns to choose a story scenario and a character type. How would the character feel in the scenario? What would they say? What might happen in the end?

Story scenario	Character type
1. You are lost in the desert trying to find water. 2. You are given a large egg. It smells a little funny and is unlike any other egg you have seen before. 3. You are going on holiday with your family, but when you arrive at your accommodation, it's not there.	1. Lazy, often bored, reckless, can't concentrate for long. 2. Organized and logical, likes to understand everything and have a plan. 3. Anxious and shy, worries about everything. Likes to be cosy and quiet.

Write notes on your favourite story scenario and character type below.

2 We can learn more about a character's personality by what they say and how they say it.

For each line of dialogue, underline the adverb used and circle the **dialogue tag**.

a "I'm so tired!" groaned Ayesha loudly.

b "I didn't want to come anyway," muttered Maryam quietly.

c "Can we just stick to the plan?" pleaded Liam desperately. "Or we'll never get there."

d "Good idea!" added Ahmad, in a friendly manner.

e "Let's just stay here," he said flatly.

3 Complete these lines of dialogue using the words in the box or your own ideas.

"According to the map, the oasis is still five miles away,"   stated   Mina.

a "But I can't walk anymore," ________________ Daniel. "My feet are killing me!"

b "Look, we can either start walking or stay here and die of thirst." ________________ Mina.

c "Fine!" ________________ Daniel. "But you're carrying the bags this time!"

d "Happy to," ________________ Mina.

4 Write a scene from a story including speech. You can use a scenario from **1** or invent your own. Remember to:
- show your different characters' personalities through what they say
- include a variety of dialogue tags.

When finished, read your scene to a partner. Can they tell what kind of characters you were trying to create?

1   Discuss with a partner what you find easy about creative writing and what you find challenging. Do any of the following apply to you?

   - "I never know how to start creative writing."
   - "I find it hard to proofread my work."
   - "My writing tends to be too short – I run out of ideas."
   - "Grammar is a problem for me."

2   Write down two things you find challenging about creative writing and give yourself some advice on how you could improve.

Something I find challenging: I find spelling difficult.

Advice: Use a dictionary to check spelling.

   a   Something I find challenging: ___________________________________

       Advice: ___________________________________

       ____

   b   Something I find challenging: ___________________________________

       Advice: ___________________________________

       ____

3   Rewrite the following text. Correct the mistakes and make any other changes you think will improve it.

> They raced onto the ~~staton~~ platform but it was to late the 4:30 train to the city train had already gone and they have missed it
>
> "What will we do now" Cam said, she was obviously upset.
>
> "We will never get to the stadium in time for the concert." Next it starts to to rain.
>
> Tam rolled his eyes Today cannot possibly get any worse he demanded

They raced onto the station platform ...

____

____

____

____

4 Improve a piece of writing you have completed in this unit. You can either rewrite the same piece and improve it, or develop the story further.

- Focus on improving the spelling, grammar and punctuation.
- Apply the advice you wrote in **2** to make your story better.

When finished, check your spelling, grammar and punctuation again. Did your advice help?

1 Discuss with a partner:

- Do you like to read reviews online before you buy or watch something?
- What are the advantages and disadvantages of online reviews?
- Can you always trust reviews that you read online?

2 Add the **evaluative adjectives** from the box to the appropriate columns in the table.

atrocious   disappointing   ordinary   charming   standard   disgusting   boring   stunning

delightful   spectacular   terrible   forgettable   satisfactory   likeable   nice   remarkable

awful   typical   pleasant   poor

Very bad	Quite bad	Neutral	Quite good	Very good
atrocious				

3 Write a 'positive' (P) or 'negative' (N) comment for each of the following things, as indicated.
Service at a restaurant (N).

The waiter took ages to come for our drinks order and then didn't tell us which things were unavailable from the menu.

a Comfort of seating at cinema (N)

b Length of wait for rides at a theme park (P)

c Value for money at a café (P)

d Cleanliness of room at a hotel (N)

4   Write a review for a restaurant, cinema, café or hotel that you know. Start with a general description. Then include three positives and three negatives. End with a rating out of ten.

When finished, circle any evaluative adjectives you have used.

1 Discuss with a partner:

- Do you ever wish you could see into the future?
- If you could find out one thing about your future life, what would it be and why?
- What are three major events in your life so far?
- What do you think you'll have completed by the time you're 25? What will you be doing at 30?

2 With a partner, discuss the difference in meaning between the pairs of sentences. Focus on the future tenses.

a When I'm 25, I'll have qualified as a doctor.

When I'm 25, I'll be qualifying as a doctor.

In sentence a, the speaker will have finished training as a doctor. But in sentence b, the speaker will still be studying and training.

b I will go to university.

I may go to university.

____

____

c When I'm 25, I'll be living abroad.

When I'm 25, I'll have lived abroad.

____

____

3 Create a timeline of your life using the sentence starters below.

Past	**Present**	**Future**
I was born . . .	I am currently . . .	I will have completed . . .
I started . . .	I enjoy . . .	I will have been to . . .
I went to . . .		I will go . . .
		I will be living . . .

NOW

4 Write a summary of your timeline. Include:

- past and present tenses
- future tenses including **future perfect** (will have done) and **future continuous** (will be doing).

When finished, underline your uses of the future perfect tense and circle your uses of the future continuous tense.

1. Discuss with a partner:
   - How do you think your teachers would describe you?
   - What positive things would they say? What negative things would they say?
   - Does your school give out school reports? What kind of information is in them? What are the benefits of school reports?

2. A **euphemism** is a less direct way of saying something. Match the word/phrase on the left to its euphemism.

died	under the weather
talks a lot	between jobs
sick/ill	passed away
unemployed	chatterbox

Do you know any more euphemisms? Discuss with a partner and write down the ones you think of.

____

____

____

3. Rewrite these negative statements to be more gentle and positive.

Maryam is awful at music and is terrible at concentrating.

Music isn't Maryam's strongest subject. She prefers to work on things in short bursts.

a. Nessa's handwriting is a complete mess!

____

b. Mohammed is lazy and makes no effort in sports lessons.

____

c. Jameel shouts out answers and doesn't put his hand up.

____

4   Write your own school report.

- Choose two subjects (perhaps your worst and best subjects).
- Write some comments about your performance – positive and negative.
- Use euphemisms.

When finished, circle the euphemisms you have used.

1 Read this newspaper article with a partner. Underline and label examples of each of the '5 Ws':

- **What** happened?
- **Where** did it happen?
- **When** did it happen?
- **Who** was involved?
- **Why** did it happen?

24 October 79

THE ROMAN TIMES

Violent Vesuvius vents fiery fury!

Vesuvius, the mighty volcano located next to the city of Pompeii in Italy, erupted yesterday causing all 12,000 residents to flee for their lives.

The eruption was catastrophic, and completely unexpected. Around 7am smoke started to drift from the mountain and local residents gathered to watch, curious as to what it might mean. There had been tremors over the previous few days, but no one knows why it erupted.

The eruption continues today. Pliny the Elder, who has been trying to help people escape by sea, reported that "ash and pieces of rock rained down … there was a darkness thicker and blacker than any night".

2 Newspaper headlines are short and dramatic in order to grab our attention. They often use **alliteration**. Write headlines for the following stories.

A pet bird alerts its family to a house fire.

Brave budgie saves family from fire!

a Sightseers notice a whale swimming in a city river.

b A small local cricket team unexpectedly beats the National team.

c A huge storm causes the electricity to be cut off for a whole city.

3   Choose one of the stories in **2**, or create your own story from one you know or something that has happened to you. Plan a newspaper article about it including the 5 Ws.

4   Write your newspaper article. Give it a headline that uses alliteration.

1 Imagine your school has asked you to plan an end-of-year event. It could be a party, a fundraising event, an awards ceremony, a sports event, a concert – something that would be successful at your school. What event would be suitable for your school? Discuss with a partner.

2 Write notes about the event you discussed in **1**.

- What is the event? Where will it be held?
- Will only students attend or parents and siblings too?
- Will there be music, food, entertainment, awards and prizes?

3 Rewrite these requests using **imperatives**.

Could you help us organize a talent show to raise money?

Help us organize a talent show to raise money.

a Would you ask everyone in the year group to suggest a song for the playlist?

b Why don't you order the food that we'll eat after the match?

c We ought to book a band to play after the awards. Perhaps we should ask them to audition first?

d Could you organize the teams?

e We need to research how much it would cost to have a speaker at the event.

4 Imagine you have gathered together the team that will help organize the event. Write a detailed plan of all the things you need to discuss. You need to:

- explain your vision for the event
- give instructions of what they need to do using imperatives.

It's important that we make this event fun for people of all ages. Let's discuss our ideas for different activities, and then write a list …

When finished, circle any imperatives you have used.

1 Discuss with a partner:
   - Do you like making things? What do you make?
   - Have you ever tried to explain how something is made?
   - How do you think the following are made: books; chocolate bars; jeans?

2 Complete these passive sentences with one of the verbs in the correct form.

| add | ~~harvest~~ | sew | heat | cut | programme |

The fruit is harvested and allowed to dry.

a The magazine pages are passed through a machine which _________________ off the edges neatly.

b The mixture is _________________ to a temperature which causes a reaction.

c Dye is _________________ to the material to make it blue.

d The computers are _________________ by specialists in China.

e The buttons are carefully _________________ on by hand.

3 Rewrite the steps below using the **passive voice**.

Fill the kettle with water from the tap.

The kettle is filled with water from the tap.

a Turn on the kettle.

____

b Take a cup and a tea bag from the cupboard.

____

c Put the tea bag in the cup.

____

d Pour boiling water into the cup.

____

e Leave the tea bag in the cup for three minutes then take it out.

____

4 Using the diagrams, write a description of how plastic bottles are recycled. Use the captions to help you but change the instructions from active to passive.

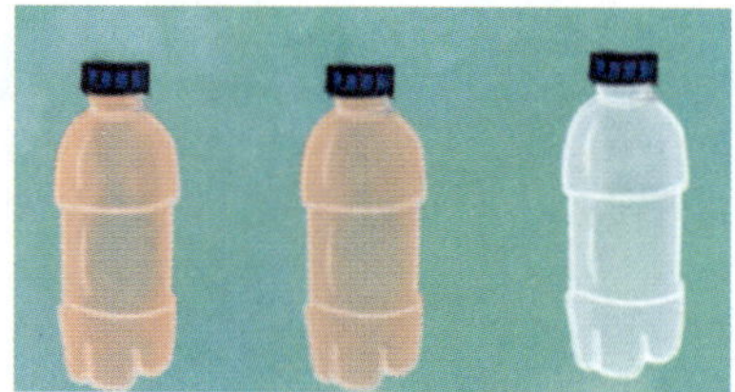

First, collect the bottles.

Remove the lids, as they are made from a different type of plastic.

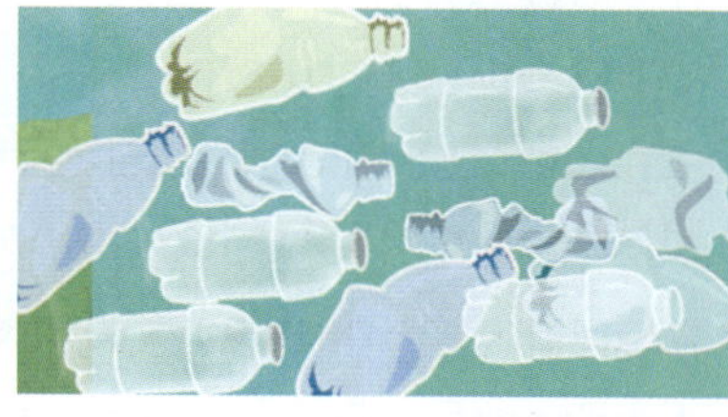

Sort the bottles to remove the coloured ones.

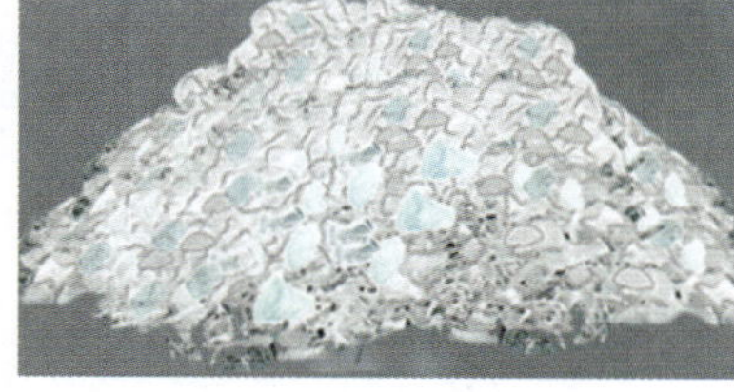

Shred the clear plastic bottles and wash the pieces.

Melt the pieces and spin them into fibres.

Turn the fibres into fleece for making clothes and blankets.

Recycling plastic bottles is a complicated process with several stages. First, the empty bottles are collected …

When finished, circle where you have used the passive voice.

1   Discuss with a partner:
- Dramatic conflict happens when characters are involved in a disagreement. Why is it important in a story?
- What are the best ways to show conflict between characters?
- Inner conflict is when a character experiences conflict within their own mind. Can you think of a story which uses this?

2   Decide if the sentences are **declarative, interrogative, exclamative** or **imperative**.

You didn't do your homework last night.   *declarative*

a   Where were you yesterday?

b   I really don't like spiders … I don't think I can walk through there.

c   What a mess!

d   Don't go that way, it's quicker through here.

e   Let's get out of here!

3   What kind of conflict (internal or external) could you introduce to these situations?

A family holiday.

One person wants to have a day at the beach but the other wants to go shopping.

a   A teenager is revising for an exam.

b   Two friends have got lost in the city and are getting hungry.

c   A group of tourists become stranded on a desert island.

4 Write a playscript that features conflict. You can use one of the situations in **3** or invent your own. Try to include at least one declarative, interrogative, imperative and exclamative sentence in the dialogue.

Mariam: What do you mean, the play's already cast?

Omar: I told you about the auditions weeks ago!

When finished, label the sentence types that you have used.

1   Discuss with a partner:
   - How do you cheer yourself up if you're feeling sad?
   - How do you cheer your friends up?
   - What kinds of stress and problems do teenagers have these days?
   - Are there ways to cheer yourself up that don't involve spending money?

2   Complete each piece of advice on how to cheer yourself up, using each of these **phrasal verbs**.

| carry on | come over | get out | give back | ~~put on~~ | set off | take up | work out |

One way to make yourself feel better is music. Put on your favourite song.

a   ________________________ to society by volunteering at a dog shelter.

b   Exercise cheers you up. It's even better if you ________________________ to music.

c   Take some water and ________________________ for a walk in the countryside.

d   You might want to stay in bed all day, but you should ________________________ doing the things you enjoy.

e   ________________________ of the house to get some fresh air.

f   Why don't you ________________________ a new hobby? Passions make us feel good.

g   Ask one of your friends to ________________________ and hang out.

3   a   Underline the phrasal verbs and circle the examples of informal language in the script below.

   Daytime, in a park.

   Hi there! Feeling a bit blue? Well, I can help you to cheer up with my favourite Top Tips!

   (holding up water bottle) Number one - look after yourself by drinking plenty of water. It helps both mind and body! So fill up your water bottle before you go out.

   Two - lace up your trainers and go out for a walk or run. Exercise boosts those feel-good endorphins.

   (stopping to greet someone) Three - don't you always feel great when you get together with a friend? Yep, of course you do!

   Four - music is a great mood booster, so put on your favourite song and dance around like nobody's watching! Awesome!

4 Write a script for a short video called 'The best ways to cheer yourself up'. Use an informal style to appeal to people your age, and try to include some phrasal verbs.

When finished, circle any phrasal verbs you have used.

1 Discuss with a partner:

- What are the main differences between a story and a poem?
- Are the following features of poems or stories, or could they be both?

  - hero
  - plot
  - dialogue
  - first person
  - **stanzas**
  - **rhyme**
  - setting
  - resolution (conclusion)

2 Two of the most common rhyme schemes in poems are AABB and ABAB. What rhyming patterns do these poems use? You can circle the rhyming words and write A or B at the end of the line to help.

Rhyming pattern: ___________

How good to lie a little while
And look up through the tree!
The Sky is like a kind big smile
Bent sweetly over me.

(Extract from 'Friends', Abbie Farwell Brown)

Rhyming pattern: ___________

An old man, going a lone highway,
Came, at the evening, cold and gray,
To a chasm, vast, and deep, and wide,
Through which was flowing a sullen tide.

(Extract from 'The Bridge Builder', Will Allen Dromgoole)

3 Think of a story or a film you know well. Break it down into the first three parts and write a sentence for each part.

a Two friends decide to set sail across the ocean.

b They are halfway across when a storm appears in the distance and begins to move closer …

c The ship is tossed and turned and eventually sinks. The two friends are left clinging to a life raft.

a Introduction: a character meets a challenge or problem.

b The difficulties increase.

c Disaster strikes: all seems lost.

4 Using the points you wrote in **3**, turn your story into a poem. Try to use rhyme if you can.

> I had a friend who loved the sea,
> He said he wanted to sail with me.
> We boarded a ship and set the course,
> But soon we faced a stormy force.
> The waves were high, the wind was strong,
> We tried to steer but all went wrong.

Share your poem with a partner. How have you both used rhyme?

1   Discuss with a partner:

    • What is the best way to show your parents, siblings or friends that you love them?

    • In films and stories, what are the typical ways characters show they love someone?

    • Can you love a place? Which places do you love?

2   An ode is a type of poem that praises a person, place or thing. Underline the examples of the **second person** in this ode and label the rhyming pattern.

> Towering mountains warmly embrace <u>you</u>. A
> Your beaches were crafted from gold. B
> Your streets are splendid; your buildings too. ____
> You spoil us with museums of old. ____
> Your parks are brimming with birds that sing ____
> Your praises. Your river shines like sapphire. ____
> No matter the season, my fair city, ____
> Summer, autumn, winter or spring, ____
> Nowhere else has more buzz, more fire, ____
> And nowhere else is as pretty. ____

3   Language in odes is often detailed, imaginative and exaggerated. For example, instead of saying 'Your eyes are wonderful', an ode might say 'Your eyes twinkle like stars in the midnight sky.'

    Read each of the following phrases from the poem and decide whether it is an example of **personification**, **alliteration**, a **simile**, a **metaphor** or **hyperbole**.

    a   Your beaches were crafted from gold. ____________________

    b   Mountains warmly embrace you. ____________________

    c   Brimming with birds that sing. ____________________

    d   Your river shines like sapphire. ____________________

    e   Nowhere else has more buzz. ____________________

    Plan some ideas for your own poem.

4 Write an ode about someone, something or somewhere you love.

- Write ten lines, and choose your rhyming pattern.
- Use a range of language features such as similes and metaphors.
- Use the second person.

1   Discuss with a partner:

- How important are settings in video games?
- Which video games have particularly good settings?
- Do you prefer bright, colourful settings or moody, dark ones?
- How can the setting affect what happens in the game?

2   In pairs, write some design notes for each of these settings. What are the main colours and landscape features? Are there any buildings? Will the characters there have props? How might the characters interact with the setting?

   a   An urban setting ______________________________

   b   An underwater setting ______________________________

   c   A futuristic setting ______________________________

3   When writing descriptions, it can be more effective to show the setting through clever use of detail, rather than simply tell the reader what's there.

   Look at each of these sentences. Which 'show' and which 'tell'?

   The warehouse is dark. tell

   The only light in the warehouse comes from flickering candles, casting strange shadows across its dirty walls. show

   a   The sun beats down on the baking concrete. ______________________________

   It is hot. ______________________________

   b   The surrounding buildings are empty. ______________________________

   Spiderwebs decorate the abandoned houses. ______________________________

   c   The snow-capped peaks tower above the plain. ______________________________

   The mountains are very high. ______________________________

   d   The garden is patterned with sweet-smelling orange and red flowers. ______________________________

   There are a lot of colourful flowers. ______________________________

4 Imagine you are creating a video game. Write a description of your setting so that a games designer can create the world for your game. Remember to:

- describe the setting, including the landscape and any buildings in it
- explain how the video game characters interact with the setting – for instance, can they dive into the water?
- use details to 'show' the setting rather than just 'tell'.

Circle an example in your writing where you 'show' rather than 'tell'.

1   Discuss with a partner:

- Do you play video games? Which ones do you enjoy?
- In what ways are video games becoming more like films?
- Can video games inspire films? Can films inspire video games?

2   Video games and films can include 'cutscenes', where the action pauses to explain part of the story. Why are cutscenes useful? Complete the sentences using the words in the box.

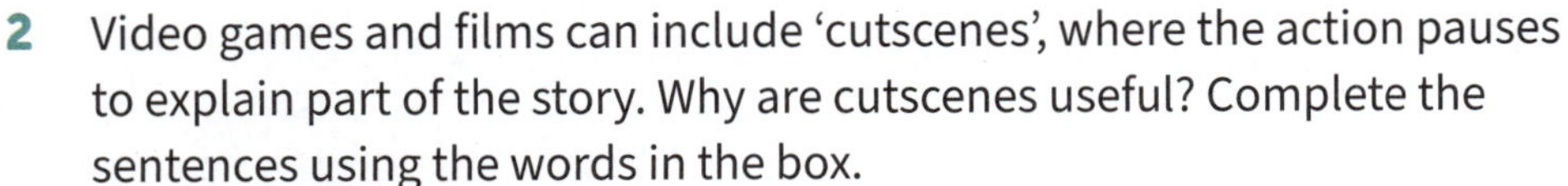

a   Cutscenes can provide some _________________________ on the character.

b   They can _________________________ the plot or set the mood.

c   Cutscenes can also define the beginning or end of a _________________________ .

d   They can be used to give the player a _________________________ .

e   Cutscenes can provide _________________________ to complete the next level or predict what might happen next in the film.

3   **a**   Read this cutscene from a video game and add the four missing **semi-colons**.

The wise old man stands in the entrance of the cave his beard and cape are blown by the wind, but he shows no sign of feeling the cold. Jem, on horseback, approaches. Ravens circle overhead.

Wise man: Ah! Hello young one. I've been expecting you. *(Jem dismounts)*

Jem: *(bowing)* I am honoured to finally meet you your power as a warrior is known throughout the land.

Wise man: I haven't always been a warrior in the past I was not so brave.

Jem: What advice would you give me?

Wise man: Find out the truth don't rest until you know.

b   Prepare to write a cutscene. It can be for a game or film you know, or something new. The cutscene should not include action, but be a conversation between two characters that provides some backstory, and perhaps other information. Make some planning notes below.

4 Write your cutscene script. Remember to include semi-colons.

5   Friends and family

1   Discuss with a partner:

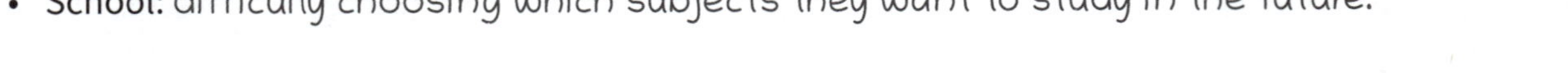

- How good are you at giving advice?
- If you had a problem, who would you ask for advice? Why?
- What problems do people ask for help with?

2   What problems could people have in the following areas?

- School: difficulty choosing which subjects they want to study in the future.

- Family: ____

- Friends: ____

- Hobbies: ____

- Neighbours: ____

3   Complete the sentences with advice for the following problems. Underline the uses of the **second conditional**.

Q: My daughter finds it hard to make friends. How can I help her?

A: That sounds very difficult. You could try encouraging her to take up a new sport or hobby where she can meet girls with similar interests.

a   **Q:** My neighbour is very noisy. What should I do?

    A: You could … ____

____

b   **Q:** My sister begged and begged for us to get a pet and now she won't look after it.

    A: I can see why you might be frustrated. If I were you, I'd … _______________

____

c   **Q:** My brother won't let me borrow his tennis raquet. He's terrible at sharing!

    A: That sounds tough. One thing you could do is … _______________

____

d   **Q:** I'm finding it hard to fall asleep at night, and I'm so tired!

    A: Hmm … if I were you, I'd … ____

____

4 Write an answer to a problem posted on a website called 'Help Me Out'. You can answer this problem, or think of another problem to give advice on. Include some second conditionals.

> If I were you, I would … You could try … It might help if you … I'd try …

Hi everyone, can anyone help me with this? When we go on holiday as a family we spend all our time arguing because we want to do different things. My daughter wants to spend all day at the beach and my son prefers shopping. We like to eat different things too, and no one likes to visit museums, which is what I prefer.

1 Discuss with a partner:

Who in your family …

- looks most like you?
- has the most similar personality to you?
- has similar tastes and interests to you?

2 Complete the sentences with an appropriate **adverb of frequency** and any other information needed. The sentences may be true for you, or not.

always	usually	sometimes	rarely	never

a My mum _________________ listens to music when cooking.

b My brother _________________ eats _________________ for breakfast.

c My grandparents _________________ bring _________________ to our house.

d My dad _________________ _________________ in the summer.

e My _________________

3 Plan your description of a family member. Add adjectives and phrases.

curly grey hair, kind eyes, always bakes me cookies, wears colourful jewellery

Likes/interests

Family member

Your relationship

Appearance/personality

Typical behaviour and habits

4 Describe your chosen family member. Use your plan from **3** and this paragraph plan to guide you. Remember to include adverbs of frequency.

Paragraph 1: appearance and personality

Paragraph 2: likes and interests, typical behaviour and habits (use adverbs of frequency)

Paragraph 3: your relationship with each other

When finished, circle the adverbs of frequency you have used.

1   Discuss with a partner:

- Who is/are your best friend(s)?
- Where is the best place to meet friends – on holiday, in your neighbourhood, at school or in clubs?
- Can a brother, sister or cousin be a best friend?
- Do you have any friends that you have lost touch with?

2   If you had a long-lost friend that you hadn't seen since you were young, what would you tell them about your life now? Note down ideas about the following subjects.

- School life: *I changed schools when we moved house four years ago.*

- Family:

- Other friends:

- Achievements:

- Interests and hobbies:

- How you have changed:

3   Circle the most appropriate verb for each sentence. Then write the name of the verb tense.

> Present simple (I am fine)   Past simple (I was hungry)   Past continuous (I was swimming yesterday)
> ~~Present perfect simple (I've eaten too much)~~   Present perfect continuous (I've been running a lot) (x2)

I haven't heard/haven't been hearing from you for so long!

I haven't heard - present perfect simple

a   I think you'd be surprised if you saw me now; I'm much taller/I was much taller.

b   When we met, I was living/have been living near the university.

c   I left/have been leaving that school last year.

d   I've been learning/I have learned French. It's going pretty well.

e   What have you been/were you doing over the last few years? Write back and tell me everything!

4 Write a letter or email to a real or imaginary friend you haven't seen for years. Tell them what you have been doing all this time and how you and your life have changed. Try to include:

- perfect tenses (I have done/I have been doing)
- past tenses (I did/I was doing)
- present tenses (I do/I am doing)

Dear Kiara,

It has been so long since we met, I thought it would be good to catch up.

When finished, underline any perfect tenses you have used.

1   Discuss with a partner:

- Are you similar or different to your friends and family members? Explain your answer.
- What do you have in common with your friends and family members? Do you like the same music, food or hobbies?
- What kind of holiday would be perfect for your best friend? What kind of holiday would your family enjoy? Would you like these holidays too?

2   A holiday itinerary is a plan of a journey, including the route and places that you want to visit. Choose the correct **modal verb** for each of these holiday itineraries.

The itinerary will/may/would start in Tortuguero. You will pick up your rental car and drive straight to La Fortuna.

a   When you arrive at the hotel, you will be treated to a four-course meal in the hotel's dining room. Or, if you prefer, you must/might/can go out to one of the city's wonderful restaurants.

b   After lunch, you would/will/have to take a boat ride on the local lake to admire the wildlife.

c   Don't forget your swimsuit; you simply could/can/must take a dip in the turquoise blue ocean.

d   We will then be exploring the forest. You must/should/will bring bug spray.

3   Imagine you are going to plan a surprise holiday for a friend or family member. Make notes under each heading:

Location: ____

____

Accommodation: ____

____

____

Food and drink: ____

____

____

Day trips / sightseeing: __________________________________

____

____

4 Write an itinerary for a surprise five-day holiday for your friend or family member. This is a dream holiday, money is no object, so be as creative as you like! Remember to include modal verbs.

| will | could | should | would | may | must | can | might |

Day 1

When finished, underline any modal verbs you have used.

1 Discuss with a partner:
- In which situations should you write more formally?
- Have you ever written a formal email or letter? What were the circumstances?
- What makes formal language different from informal language?

2 Vague language (language that is not clear or not detailed) is a feature of informal English. The vague language in each sentence has been underlined. Can you suggest something more specific to replace it? Use the words and phrases below or your own ideas.

belongings   Five hundred   guests   Miami   that this liquid is an acid   the second tab

I need to move all my <u>stuff</u>. *belongings*

a The <u>people at the wedding</u> filed into the church. _______________

b <u>A lot of</u> students are interested in taking this course. _______________

c Click on <u>that thing there</u>. _______________

d There was a significant amount of flooding in <u>that place</u>. _______________

e This experiment teaches us <u>something</u>. _______________

3 Match the informal expression with a more formal one.

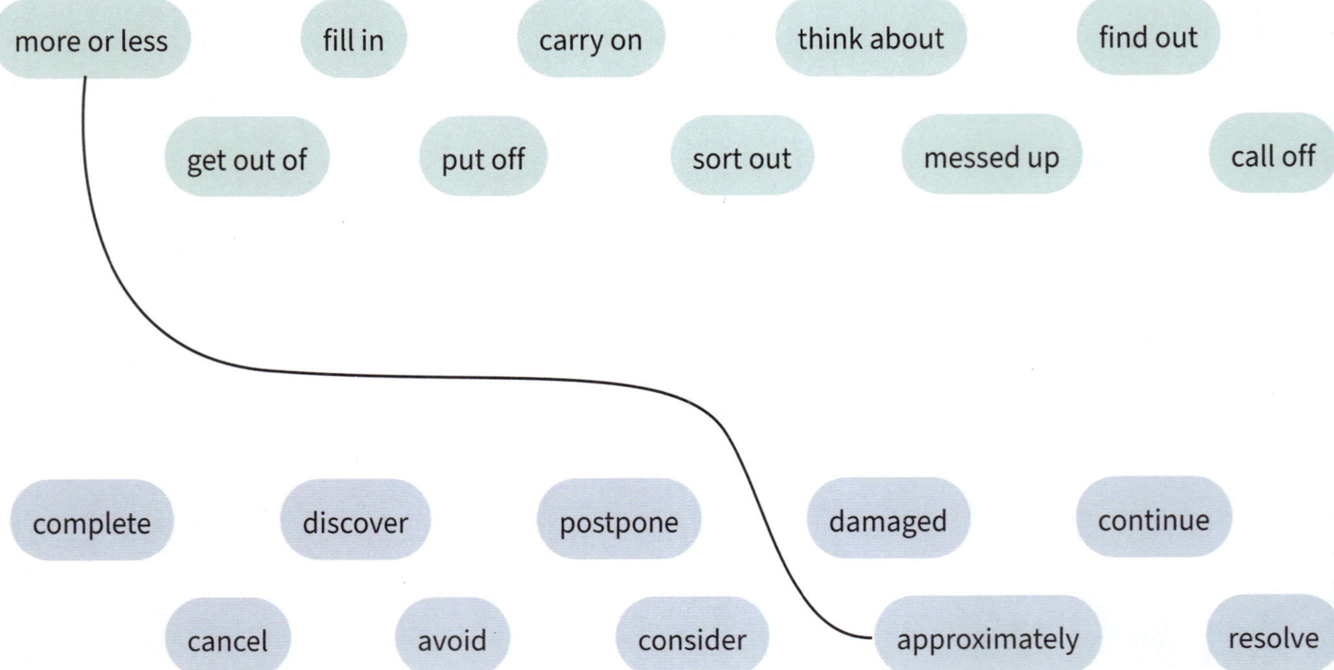

4 Write an email to your teacher. Apologize for missing a class and tell your teacher that you have attached some work for them to check and provide feedback on.

- Use formal vocabulary and try to avoid vague or unclear language.
- Write a topic in the subject box such as 'Today's class'.
- Remember to be polite.

Subject:

When finished, circle three words or phrases that are formal.

1   Do you have any funny stories about things that have gone wrong with family or friends? Talk to a partner.

2   Complete the phrases in these sentences. All of them use either 'in' or 'on'.

We all know who is in charge here – the boss!

a   I'm sorry – I didn't do it ____________ purpose.

b   When he was chosen for the school football team, he was ____________ cloud nine.

c   I will get ____________ trouble if I don't clean up this mess.

d   I can't believe I forgot Aisha's name; it was ____________ the tip of my tongue.

e   I can't talk now; I'm ____________ a hurry.

f   I'm sorry to rain ____________ your parade, but the car is broken, we're not going anywhere.

g   Nobody wanted to mention Ravi's new haircut. It was the elephant ____________ the room.

h   Luckily my dad was ____________ hand to help us clear up the mess.

3   Plan to write about a funny disaster. It could be something you talked about in **1** or something made up. What might you both have said? You can use some of the **colloquial** phrases in **2** to help you, or think of your own.

4 Write about a funny disaster using colloquial language.

When finished, circle the phrases that use 'in' or 'on'.

1 Using these topics as a starting point, describe to a partner something that annoys you. Why does it annoy you? Give lots of detail. Next, describe something you love and explain why.

2 Fill in the gaps with the emotive words below.

~~incredibly~~ repetitive infuriating

cherished overcome gentle

books, TV and films

technology

travel

food

sport

the weather

Let's face it. This sport is   *incredibly*   boring.

a These ______________________ people simply stop in the middle of the street to check their mobile phones!

b The ______________________ breeze on your face as you stroll through a sunny park fills me with peace and calm.

c Sport inspires us to ______________ challenges, achieve our most ______________ goals and celebrate victories.

d Everywhere you go, ______________ adverts are trying to sell you something!

3 Describe some of the things you love and hate using **emotive language**. You can use the words below to help.

relaxing   interesting   disgusting   fills me with happiness   drives me mad

gets on my nerves   noisy   serene   fulfilling   doesn't make sense   strange

Dropping litter is selfish, disgusting and is destroying the environment.

____

____

____

____

____

____

4 Write a short article about what you love and hate and try to persuade the reader that they should agree with you. Use emotive language to persuade them.

Do you know what really gets on my nerves? … / Don't you just love it when … ?

When finished, underline any emotive language you have used.

1   Discuss with a partner. What do you like about your country? Make notes about what you like and why.

I like the beaches because they're clean and not too crowded.

2   Add the correct **co-ordinating conjunction** to each sentence.

and	nor	~~but~~	or	so

The shopping centres can be really busy, but if you go late in the day, they are usually quieter.

a   We have really peaceful countryside _____________ we have more lively areas.

b   If you fancy some culture, you could visit one of the many art museums _____________ you could try an outdoor sculpture park.

c   Fortunately, we don't have a big problem with litter _____________ do we have a problem with graffiti.

d   It can be very hot in summer _____________ bring suncream and a hat!

3   Write multi-clause sentences about your country using **subordinating conjunctions**.

despite	when	even though	because	if	although	until

If you come in summer, remember to pack cool clothes.

____

____

____

____

____

4   You have been asked to write an article for a tourism website. They would like you to promote all the positive things about your country and offer advice to visitors. Use multi-clause sentences.

Welcome! I know you're going to have a great time here. In order to get the most out of your visit, you should ...

When finished, underline the conjunctions in your work.

1   Discuss with a partner:
- What are some of your favourite products? Think about clothes, footwear, food and cosmetics.
- How many different ways are there of marketing a product or brand?
- How could email or text messages be used to market a brand?

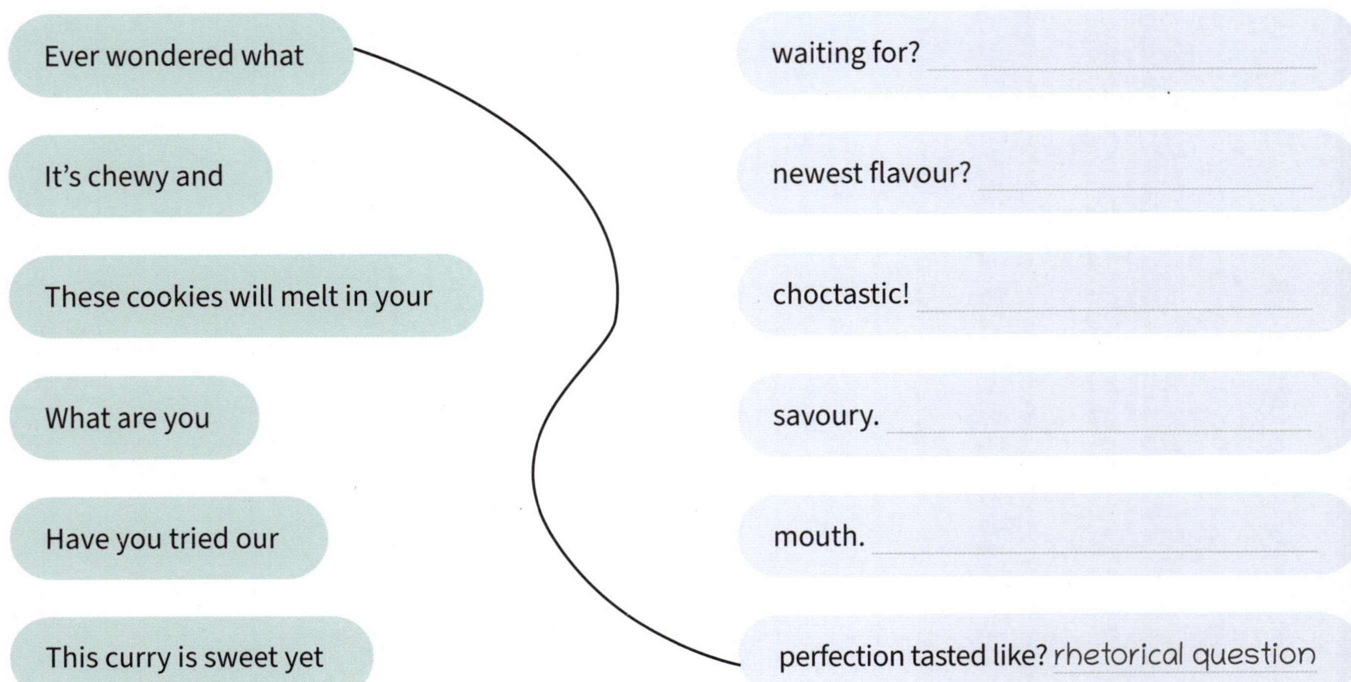

2   Promotional writing often uses **alliteration** and **rhetorical questions**.
Match the sentence parts. Then write if each one is alliteration or a rhetorical question.

Ever wondered what	waiting for?
It's chewy and	newest flavour?
These cookies will melt in your	choctastic!
What are you	savoury.
Have you tried our	mouth.
This curry is sweet yet	perfection tasted like? *rhetorical question*

3   Choose one of the products you discussed in **1** and write positive phrases or sentences about it using alliteration and rhetorical questions.

stylish sustainable sandals / Wouldn't you like to follow fashion AND protect the planet?

4 Imagine you are part of the company's marketing team helping to launch the product. Write a promotional email.

- What is your product? What are its best/most interesting features?
- Use the email subject box to write a header to get the reader's attention.
- Try to include alliteration and rhetorical questions.

Subject:

When finished, circle any alliteration you have used and underline any rhetorical questions.

1 Discuss with a partner:
   - Does your school have a debate team? If so, would you like to join it? If not, would you like there to be one?
   - What skills can students learn by debating?
   - What are some good topics for debates?

2 Imagine you are preparing for this debate: 'Should all students be required to do community service?' Which debate technique is used in each sentence?

emotive language	facts	**inclusive language**	~~introduction~~
	power of three	**rhetorical questions**	

It is our position that students should not have to complete community service; they have more than enough to do with school, friends and family life. Introduction

   a This planet is our precious home, protecting it should be our top priority!

   b Did you know that 75% of young people are happy to have completed

      community service?

   c Community service will provide students with valuable skills to add to their CVs,

      a social network and a boost to their health.

   d Community service could be good for us all.

   e Do you really want to see young people spending their formative years cleaning the streets

      instead of learning about science, maths and language?

3 You are going to have a debate with your partner. Decide which topic you will debate and who will argue **yes** and who will argue **no**.
   - Should wild animals be kept in captivity? Yes/No
   - Should sport be compulsory in school until the age of 18? Yes/No
   - Should we be allowed to eat exactly what we want? Yes/No
   - Is being happy the most important thing in life? Yes/No

Working separately, complete the table. Try to use facts and emotive language in your notes.

Overview of your argument:

My three main arguments	My opponent's potential arguments	My counter arguments

4   Now hold your debate with your partner. When finished, review the debate techniques in **2**. How many did you use?

1   Tell a partner about a book, film, sport, interest or food that you like but that your partner doesn't like. What are the things you like about it?

2   Match the beginnings and ends of these **conditional sentences**.

You'll love hockey,	you'll still be gripped by the sequel.
As long as you don't have trouble sleeping,	if you like running and contact sports.
Even if you haven't seen the first film,	you should definitely try this recipe!
Unless you have an allergy,	that you take safety seriously.
Rock climbing is very safe on the condition	you'll love this scary novel!

3   Write persuasive sentences about your chosen topic in **1** using the following devices.

Rhetorical question

Have you ever wondered what happiness tastes like?

a   **Power of three**

b   Use of facts and statistics

c   Appeal to the emotions

d   **Alliteration**

e Imperatives

4 Now it's time to persuade your partner. Write a speech to persuade them to share your view of your topic from **1** and **3**.

- Use conditionals such as 'you will', 'if', 'as long as', 'even if', 'unless' and 'on the condition that' to draw your partner in.
- Use other persuasive devices, such as those from **3**.

e Imperatives

Read your speech to your partner. Did you manage to persuade them?

1 You're going to write a script for a TV advert promoting one of these crazy products. Talk to a partner about which one you would choose.

- Umbrella mate: The hands-free flying umbrella that protects from rain or sun!
- Lunch hat: With this hat, you'll always have a snack within easy reach!
- Hover scooter: Avoid the crowds with this flying scooter!

2 Match the **similes** to their meanings. What adverts could they be used in?

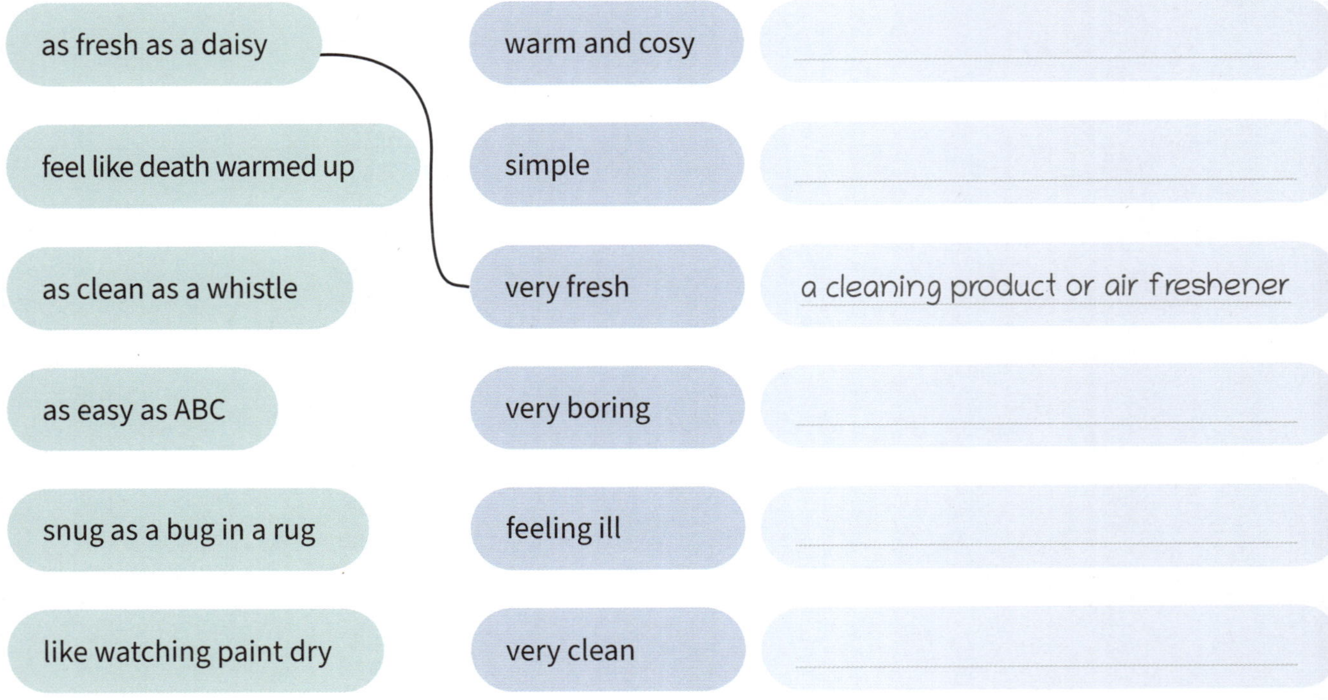

as fresh as a daisy	warm and cosy	
feel like death warmed up	simple	
as clean as a whistle	very fresh	a cleaning product or air freshener
as easy as ABC	very boring	
snug as a bug in a rug	feeling ill	
like watching paint dry	very clean	

3 Think of ideas to advertise your chosen product. Can you include any similes?

4 Create a storyboard and script for your TV advert. Sketch what you want to appear on screen and add the advertising script alongside. Remember to include similes.

Do you feel like you're in an oven, slowly roasting in the fierce sun? Or is it like a giant magnifying glass is focusing its heat on your head?

abstract noun an emotion, feeling, quality or idea you cannot see, touch, taste or smell.
- **Friendship** was important to Ana.
- Rashid felt **anger** towards his brother.

adverbs of time add information to verbs, adjectives, other adverbs or whole sentences. Adverbs of time tell us **when** the action happened.
- We finished work **earlier**.

adverbs of frequency add information to verbs, adjectives, other adverbs or whole sentences. Adverbs of frequency tell us **how often** the action happens.
- **Sometimes** we have pizza for tea.

alliteration when two or more words start with the same sound and are used in the same sentence.
- It was a **s**low, **s**ad, **s**orrowful song.

colloquialism a well-known expression mostly used in informal speech. It's a type of figurative language, and its meaning is different from its literal meaning. It can also be classified as an idiom.
- She wasn't born yesterday! (She's not gullible)

concrete noun something you can touch, such as a person, an animal, a place or a thing.
- **dog, cat, student, book, house**

conditional tense shows that one action depends on another (there is a condition). Conditional words are words like **if, as long as, providing that**.
- **If we finish** our work, **we can go** to the park.

conjunction a linking word. **Co-ordinating conjunctions** join two parts of a sentence that make sense on their own. The co-ordinating conjunctions are **for, and, nor, but, or, yet, so**. **Subordinating conjunctions** join extra information to the main clause. Some examples are **if, as, although, because, when, until**.
- I finished my homework **so** I could go to the park.
- **When** he went to the shops, he ran.

declarative sentence a statement.
- I am a keen artist.

dialogue tag a phrase, generally at the start or end of direct speech. A dialogue tag indicates who is speaking.
- "Did you get my text?" **asked Mum**.

emotive language the language writers use to create an emotional response in the reader. It is often used in persuasive writing or to make readers sympathize with a character.

euphemism a polite word or phrase that is used to avoid saying something harsh, uncomfortable or even offensive.
- they exchanged words (instead of 'they had an argument').

evaluative adjectives words that judge the thing they are describing. The judgement can be positive or negative.
- It was a **wonderful** show.

exclamative sentence expresses a strong emotion and ends with an exclamation mark.
- I won!

future continuous tense describes an ongoing action that will occur in the future.
- Hopefully, they **will be making** dinner by then.
- We **will be eating** when you arrive.

future perfect tense describes an action that will have been completed at some point in the future.
- Hopefully, they **will have made** dinner by then.
- We **will have eaten** before you arrive.

hyperbole when writers use exaggeration for effect. It draws attention to the point they are making and can add humour. Hyperbole is a type of figurative language.
- She's **as old as the hills**.

imperative gives a command or instruction. The imperative verb tells you what to do. Often, the verb is the first word in the sentence. The subject is understood to be 'you'.
- **Tidy** your room.
- **Add** the water **carefully**.

inclusive language when inclusive pronouns (**we, our**) are used to encourage people to engage with what is being said. It is often used in persuasive writing.
- **We** must work together to create a better future for our children.

interrogative sentence asks a question and ends with a question mark.
- Have you seen my bag?

irregular plural noun when there is more than one of the noun. Regular plurals end in 's' (**tables, forests, shoes**). Irregular plurals do not end in 's' (**feet, children, men**).
- The **women** saw plenty of **sheep** in the fields.

language devices techniques writers use to effectively communicate a mood, feeling or theme. Sometimes, they are used to compare things or make vivid images and sounds for the reader. Some of the most common language devices are **simile, metaphor, alliteration, personification** and **hyperbole**.

- Simile: My hands are **as cold as ice**.
- Metaphor: The snow **was a great white carpet**.
- Alliteration: **Sh**e sells **sh**iny **sh**oes in her small **sh**op.
- Personification: The flowers **danced in the wind**.
- Hyperbole: This homework **will take forever**.

metaphor a way of describing something by saying it is something else. It's sometimes called a figure of speech, and it is a type of figurative language.

- Thanks for your help. **You are a star**!

modal verbs show different levels of possibility or certainty (**must, will, can, might, may, can't, won't, should, could, would**).

- I **could** lend you my textbook if you need it.
- I **will** lend you my textbook.

passive voice when the object (person or thing having the verb done to it) appears before the verb. The subject (person or thing that does the verb) appears after the verb or not at all. The emphasis is on the object (person or thing having the verb done to it).

- The **cat was chased** by the **dog**.
- The **letter will be returned**.

past continuous tense describes an ongoing activity in the past. It can be used to set the scene for another action.

- They **were making** dinner when I arrived.

past perfect tense describes something that happened, or was happening, before a particular event in the past.

- They **had played** football. (past perfect simple)
- They **had been playing** football. (past perfect continuous)

personification a way of describing something that is not human by giving it human characteristics.

- The storm **raged** overhead.

phrasal verb a verb combined with a preposition or an adverb to give a different meaning. For example, the verb *grow* usually means to become larger or increase in amount, but the phrasal verb *grow up* means to become an adult.

- My sister is **growing up** fast.

power of three when the writer uses three points, three sentence patterns, or a list of three to emphasise their point. It is a technique often used in persuasive writing.

- We have poured our **blood, sweat** and **tears** into this project.

preposition a word that tells us where, when or in which direction something is.

- The book is **on** the shelf.
- We'll come back **after** lunch.

present perfect tense describes something that started in the past but still affects, or continues into, the present.

- She **has drawn** the first sketch.
- I **have been cooking** dinner.

proper noun name of a particular person, event, place or thing. Proper nouns begin with a capital letter.

- **Freddie, Paris, Jupiter**

relative clause adds more information to the noun. It begins with a relative pronoun (who, whom, whose, which, that) or a relative adverb (when, where, why). It does not make sense on its own.

- The book **that we bought today** is fascinating.
- The book, **which he wrote last year**, is said to be the author's best work.

rhetorical questions are asked to make a point rather than to get an answer. They are often used in persuasive writing.

- Who wants to swim in a sea full of plastic?

rhyme when two or more words have a word ending that sounds similar. Rhyming words are often found at the ends of lines of poetry or song lyrics. Rhyme is sometimes used in advertising.

- In winter I get up at **night**
  And dress by yellow candle-**light**
  (Bed in Summer, by Robert Louis Stevenson)

second conditional used to imagine a future situation that may be unlikely. It uses **if** + **past simple** + **would** + **infinitive**.

- **If** I **were** you, **I would find out** about after-school clubs or classes.

second person when the text is written from the reader's viewpoint (you, your).

- **You** like going to the beach.
- **You** were tired that evening, so **you** went to bed early.

semi-colon a punctuation mark with a few different uses. It can join items on a list that already contains commas. It can link two closely related independent clauses. It can create a smooth transition into an independent clause that starts with a connective.

- We bought burgers, buns and ketchup; a selection of cakes and ice cream; and plenty of soft drinks.
- There were five slices of cake this morning; now there are none.
- It was freezing; however, everyone seemed to enjoy themselves.

simile a way of describing something by comparing it to something else. It is a type of figurative language. Similes use the words 'as' or 'like'.

- The sun is **like a yellow beach ball**.

stanza a set of lines grouped together to divide a poem into separate parts. It gives a poem structure, just as a paragraph structures prose.

third person uses the pronouns **he, she, his, her, their, them**. It is written from the point of view of the person or people being talked about. In a third person subjective narrative, the narrator has access to the thoughts and feelings of just some of the characters. In a third person omniscient narrative, the narrator is all-knowing. They can see into the minds of every character.

- Subjective: **He** was unable to read the look on her face.
- Omniscient: **They** sat down to discuss it. Mali hoped no one could see how embarrassed **she** was, and Carlos wished **he** were anywhere else.

uncountable nouns people, places, animals or things. Most nouns are countable nouns, which can be singular or plural (dog/dogs). Uncountable nouns do not have a plural form (rice, music, information).

- Please help yourselves to the **rice**.